Navigating The Job Maze

Uncovering the Secret Routes to Professional Success

By

Bobby Castro

Table of Contents

Introduction

Finding your road to professional success can frequently feel like navigating a perilous maze in the dynamic modern job market. You have a plethora of options in front of you, each with its chances, difficulties, and rewards. You can feel overwhelmed, unsure of where to go, and secretly long for a hidden map that can lead you to your ultimate career destination as you enter this maze of choices.

We're glad you're here to learn about "Navigating the Job Maze: Uncovering the Secret Routes to Professional Success." We begin on an exciting journey together in this book as we solve the mysteries of the job market and expose the secret routes that can help you achieve the height of your professional ambitions. We set out to simplify the process of career navigation and equip you with the skills and knowledge you need to succeed by drawing on the experiences of many successful people as well as the knowledge of career specialists.

Not your normal career guide, this one. We don't support general guidance that simply touches the surface or a one-size-fits-all philosophy. Instead, we examine the seldom-explored corners and secret passageways deep into the complex web of the work maze. True professional success rarely results from following the beaten route, therefore we find alternative tactics, expose unorthodox success stories, and refute conventional thinking.

You can unlock your entire potential by using the keys found on these pages. We discuss the significance of self-awareness and how knowing your special talents, interests, and values may help you navigate your life's journey. We go into the art of networking, which is more than just a cursory handing out of business cards. It is a potent means of creating real relationships that can open doors and influence your professional path.

But this is not where our trip ends. We dispel common misconceptions about the job search process and offer expert advice on how to write a compelling CV, ace interviews, and stand out from the competition. We look into the ways to improve professionally and shed light on the frequently hidden routes that can help you reach new heights.

"Navigating the Job Maze" is your reliable guide whether you're a new graduate entering the job market for the first time, an experienced professional trying to change careers, or anyone wishing to maximize their potential in the workplace. It is a route plan laced with motivation, useful guidance, and true tales of overcoming adversity.

So, are you prepared to set out on this amazing journey? Together, we will decipher the enigmas of the job maze and reveal the hidden paths to success in the workplace. It's time to take charge of your career, overcome the obstacles in your way, and come out on top. The journey has begun!

Chapter 1

Welcome to the Dynamic World of Job Hunts

Congratulations! By stepping into the exciting world of job searches, you have already begun the process of defining your career. In this chapter, we'll examine the dynamic job-search environment and provide you with useful tips and techniques to deal with any obstacles you might run into. This chapter will give you the necessary tools to be successful in your job search, whether you are a recent graduate, an established professional looking for new chances, or someone making a career change.

Recognizing the Employment Market

The job market is a sophisticated and dynamic ecosystem that is affected by societal, technological, and economic developments. Understanding the variables at play is essential for successfully modifying your job search strategy.

1. Economic Trends: Pay attention to economic statistics including unemployment rates, GDP growth, and forecasts for particular industries. You can use these indicators to find industries that are growing and are likely to have a greater need for qualified workers.

2. Emerging Industries: Job opportunities grow along with the emergence of new technology and industries. Keep up with the most recent developments in fields including biotechnology, blockchain, renewable energy, and artificial intelligence. Targeting growing sectors can be more successful if you can anticipate these transitions.

Create a Professional Profile

Your talents, expertise, and personal brand are all represented on your professional profile. By optimizing it, you will greatly increase your chances of standing out from the crowd.

1. Resume/CV: Create an appealing resume or curriculum vitae that showcases your pertinent credentials, successes, and accomplishments. Create a unique resume for each job application, highlighting your qualifications and achievements that are relevant to the position.

2. Online Presence: In the current digital era, having a presence online is crucial. Make a LinkedIn profile that highlights your qualifications, passions, and recommendations. Pay attention to your other social media accounts because prospective employers frequently look at them as well.

3. Networking: For job seekers, networking is a powerful tool. Get in touch with people who can provide insights, recommendations, or even job chances by going to industry events, joining professional groups, and using internet platforms.

Job Search Techniques

A deliberate strategy is necessary to find the ideal employment. Searching employment boards by yourself might not produce the greatest results. To streamline your job search, take into account the following tactics:

1. Job Boards and Aggregators: Check out well-known employment boards and aggregators to identify pertinent jobs. Set up email alerts and modify your search criteria to receive notifications of new listings.

2. Company websites: Before publishing job openings on external platforms, many organizations prefer

to post them on their websites. Do some research and frequently check out the career pages of companies that interest you.

3. Professional Networks: Use your connections to find out about unlisted employment openings. Your friends, relatives, and past coworkers may be able to introduce you to hiring managers or refer you to relevant openings if you let them know about your job search objectives.

4. Recruiters and Staffing Agencies: Connect with recruiters and staffing firms that are experts in your industry. These experts can offer helpful advice throughout the

employment process and have access to untapped job markets.

Adapting to a Changing Environment

Technology, automation, and globalization are all driving factors in the ongoing evolution of the labor market. The secret to being current and competitive is adaptation.

1. Persistent Learning: To keep on top of trends, invest in ongoing education and skill development. Attend workshops, sign up for online courses, and earn certifications to expand your expertise and show

prospective employers that you have a growth attitude.

2. Remote Work and the Gig Economy: Traditional job arrangements have changed as a result of the growth of remote work and the gig economy. Accept the freedom that remote work offers and look into side jobs to build your professional network and obtain useful experience.

Welcome to the exciting world of job searching, where there are many opportunities yet tough competition. You may confidently move through this dynamic environment by having a solid professional profile, being aware of the job market, using efficient job search techniques, and being flexible. Remember that choosing the perfect career path requires persistence and that every job search is a learning experience. Wishing you luck as you travel!

Chapter 2

Job Hunting is Challenging: Seven Powerful Strategies to Succeed

Finding a job may be a difficult and overwhelming process. It's essential to arm yourself with powerful techniques to set yourself apart from the competition and land your dream job in today's constantly changing employment market. This chapter will examine seven effective techniques that will improve your job search process and raise your chances of success.

1. Specify your Career Objectives:

Spend some time defining your career goals before starting your job search. Choose the position you desire, the industry you want to work in, and the necessary skills and certifications. This clarity will enable you to customize your job search and concentrate on positions that are in line with your goals.

2. Create a Strong Resume:

Potential employers' first impression of you will come from your resume. It should succinctly convey your pertinent experiences, accomplishments, and talents. Create a unique resume for each job application, highlighting the abilities and credentials required by that particular employer. Quantify your accomplishments, include action verbs, and make sure your CV is flawless and well-written.

3. Establish a Powerful Online Presence:

Having a good online presence is essential in the current digital era. Make a polished LinkedIn profile that highlights your qualifications and work history. Make connections with professionals in your field, join pertinent organizations, and take an active role in conversations. Consider building a personal website or portfolio as well to display your achievements.

4. Network Successfully:

In the job search process, networking is essential. To meet people in your target field, go to conferences, career fairs, and industry events. Ask your friends, family, and former classmates for introductions and recommendations. Maintain a professional internet profile, participate in worthwhile conversations, and develop connections that may result in employment prospects.

5. Focus On One Job At A Time:

Don't apply to every job you see; instead, prioritize quality over quantity. Find businesses that share your beliefs and professional ambitions. Adapt your applications to each position, demonstrating your familiarity with the business and how your abilities may help it succeed. Use online job boards, corporate websites, and job search engines to uncover possibilities that are relevant to you.

6. Get Ready for Interviews By:

The first step in getting a job is having an interview. Do a thorough investigation of the business, its culture, and the position you're looking for. Prepare succinct, persuasive responses to typical interview questions by practicing them. Display your passion, expertise, and capacity to support the goals of the firm. Prepare intelligent interview questions as well to show the interviewer that you are interested and engaged.

7. Build Perseverance and Resilience:

Job searching can be an up-and-down experience with its fair share of failures and rejections. To maintain motivation throughout the process, it is imperative to cultivate resilience and persistence. Take advice from each rejection, grow from it, and make the required adjustments. Keep a cheerful attitude, stick to a schedule, and ask your friends and family for guidance and support.

Although looking for a job might be difficult, by using these seven effective tactics, you can greatly improve your chances of success.

Define your professional objectives, create a standout CV, establish a solid web presence, successfully network, customize your job search, get ready for interviews, and develop resiliency and tenacity. Remember that you can successfully navigate the job market and land the position you've been striving toward with the appropriate methods and a proactive attitude.

Chapter 3

How To Take On Any Difficulties You Face During A Job Search

Finding a job may be a difficult and frequently overwhelming process. Along the road, challenges and hurdles are commonplace. However, if you have the correct attitude and tools, you may get through these obstacles and find success in your job search. We'll cover efficient strategies and useful pointers in this chapter to assist you in overcoming any challenges you might run into during job hunting.

1. Develop a Positive Attitude:

When experiencing challenges in your job search, it's essential to keep an optimistic outlook. Keep in mind that setbacks are just transitory and can present learning opportunities. Maintain your confidence in your talents while concentrating on your accomplishments and qualities. Be in the company of upbeat, encouraging people who will inspire you when things are tough.

2. Recognize and Remove Obstacles:

It's critical to pinpoint the precise obstacles preventing your job hunt from moving forward. Lack of necessary skills, a lack of networking opportunities, or a competitive job market are examples of common obstacles. Create a strategy to overcome these challenges after you have identified them. This could entail learning new skills through education or training, growing your professional network through meetups or online communities, or investigating employment options in various cities or sectors.

3. Develop Your Talents:

Being competitive in the work market requires ongoing learning and skill development. Spend time learning or developing the talents that are in great demand in the field you want to enter. Utilize the online training, workshops, and certifications that can improve your resume and position you as a more desirable prospect to employers.

4. Develop a Strategic Network:

Finding career prospects requires a lot of networking. By participating in industry events, joining pertinent online groups, and contacting other experts in your sector, you may grow your professional network. Create lasting connections by putting others' needs and wants before your own by being helpful and valuable to them. The benefits of networking include useful introductions, knowledge of job opportunities, and even mentorship opportunities.

5. Polish the Materials For Your Application:

Your marketing materials for the job search process are your résumé, cover letter, and web profiles. Spend some time customizing your application materials to each job's particular criteria. Draw attention to your accomplishments, experiences, and talents that are pertinent to the position. Make sure your writing is flawless, organized, and effectively conveys your qualifications.

6. Interviewing practice:

Although practice makes perfect, interviews can be nerve-wracking. Prepare thoughtful and succinct answers to frequent interview questions by doing some research. To mimic real-world situations, hold mock interviews with friends or family members. Make a note of your advantages and weaknesses, then attempt to improve your body language, communication, and interview performance as a whole.

7. Ask for Advice and Take Advice from Rejections:

Being rejected is a common occurrence during the job-seeking process. Make the most of them as chances to learn and advance rather than focusing on them. Request input from potential employers or interviewers to learn about areas where you may improve. Examine your previous applications and interviews to look for trends or areas that could want improvement. As you obtain feedback, modify your strategies in response, and keep improving your strategy until you are successful.

The job search process might be arduous, but with the appropriate attitude, approaches, and persistence, you can get through any obstacles you come across. Develop a positive outlook, recognize and remove obstacles, continually improve your talents, strategically network, improve your application materials, practice interviews, and get feedback from rejections. By using these strategies, you will improve your chances of locating a rewarding career that matches your objectives and desires. Keep in mind that every obstacle you overcome presents a chance for development and advancement.

Chapter 4

Ways to Decide on a Profession or Obtain Employment

Choosing a career and finding work can be difficult tasks in the fast-paced and competitive world of today. This chapter attempts to offer advice and methods to aid people in making wise career selections and successfully navigating the employment market. The parts that follow will provide you with insightful information and useful tips, whether you are a recent graduate, thinking about a career shift, or looking for your first job.

1. Self-evaluation and reflection:

It is crucial to reflect on and evaluate oneself before starting a career route. Recognize your values, interests, and strengths to find suitable careers that fit your goals and desires. Consider performing self-evaluation exercises, such as personality, skill, and career aptitude exams. For more perspectives and insights into your skills and potential career paths, ask for input from mentors, friends, and family.

2. Investigation and Research

Spend time researching and exploring different careers after you are more aware of your interests and skills. Learn more about various industries, job responsibilities, and market trends by using online resources, career portals, and professional networks. Conduct informational interviews with professionals in your area of interest to learn more about their workdays, educational requirements, and career growth from their perspectives. To build your network and learn useful knowledge, go to workshops, conferences, and career fairs.

3. Part-time Employment, Volunteer Work, and Internships:

Your employability will increase dramatically if you have practical experience, and it will also give you important insights into potential career options. Look for internships, volunteer positions, or part-time employment in fields or organizations that interest you. In addition to exposing you to real-world situations, these experiences also give you the chance to develop and display transferrable talents and make new connections in the professional world.

They can also assist you in reinforcing your career decisions or, if necessary, changing your focus.

4. Education and Professional Development:

Maintaining competitiveness in the employment market requires ongoing professional growth. Determine what talents you need to gain or develop, and then think about seeking further education or certifications in those areas. To increase your expertise and show that you are dedicated to your professional development, attend workshops, seminars, and webinars in your area of interest. Join organizations and groups in your field to gain access to resources, networking opportunities, and training tailored to your field.

5. Mentoring and Networking

When looking for jobs, having a strong professional network is essential. Attend industry-specific events, sign up for social media groups for professionals, and make connections with people who have professional interests. Create connections with mentors who can offer support, direction, and guidance throughout your career journey. Attend networking events, job fairs, and informative interviews to meet businesspeople and widen your network. Don't forget to keep up a professional online image and use resources like LinkedIn to interact with possible jobs.

6. Job Search Techniques

A successful job search approach is crucial while trying to land a job. For each position you apply for, create a strong CV and cover letter showing your relevant experience and talents. Utilize company websites, internet job boards, and networking sites for professionals to look into job possibilities. Inquire about possible career prospects through your network and think about utilizing the strength of personal connections, too.

When preparing for interviews, learn about the business, practice answering typical interview questions, and successfully present your qualifications.

Selecting a career and finding work need careful thought, introspection, and strategic planning. People can increase their chances of making wise career decisions and finding meaningful employment prospects by doing self-evaluation, research, acquiring real-world experience, and developing strong networks. Keep in mind that career paths can vary and evolve, so be flexible, value lifelong learning, and pursue your professional objectives actively.

Chapter 5

The Five Wage Negotiation Secrets

A crucial component of every job search or professional growth is wage negotiation. It requires striking a careful balance between proving your value and upholding a good working relationship with your company. This chapter will provide five strategies for effective pay negotiations, giving you the authority to get paid what you are due.

Secret 1: Recognize Your Worth

To be successful in any negotiation, it's essential to know your market value. Investigate market norms, pay scales for comparable roles, and the particular requirements of your position. Take into account your successes, talents, and experience, all of which add to your value as an employee. Knowing your value enables you to successfully express your demands during negotiations.

Secret 2: Build a Strong Case

A convincing case serves as the cornerstone of a successful

negotiation. Create a persuasive argument that highlights your accomplishments, your contributions to the business, and any special abilities or qualifications that make you stand out. Give specific examples of how your work has improved the bottom line of the company. By supporting your claims with facts, you may strengthen your case and improve your negotiating position.

Secret 3: Concentrate on Mutual Gain

Successful talks aim for a win-win result. Instead of taking a combative stance, stress the advantages that an improved wage can provide for both sides. Emphasize how your increased salary might boost loyalty, productivity, and motivation. Show how the company's long-term goals are compatible with investing in your progress. You improve the chances of a successful conclusion by framing the negotiation as a team effort.

Secret 4: Take Advantage of Extra Perks and Benefits

Even while income is a sizable part of compensation, it is not the only thing to take into account. Explore additional perks and advantages that might enhance your entire package by looking beyond the base salary. Consider bargaining for a flexible schedule, chances for professional growth, performance incentives, equity, or improved healthcare coverage. You can find innovative solutions that meet both your financial and non-financial demands by extending the discussion.

Secret 5: Be an Expert Communicator

The secret to a successful pay negotiation is effective communication. Engage in active listening to your employer's viewpoint, taking note of their issues and constraints. Keep your composure and speak with an authoritative tone that doesn't border on aggression. Practice guiding the conversation with effective negotiation strategies including framing, mirroring, and open-ended inquiries. Keep in mind that tone of voice and body language is also very important when communicating.

Wage negotiating is an art that calls for planning, a plan of attack, and strong communication abilities. You can improve your odds of succeeding by following the five strategies covered in this chapter: recognizing your value, putting together a strong case, concentrating on mutual gain, utilizing extra benefits, and mastering communication. Always keep in mind that respect, cooperation, and a mutual understanding of shared objectives are the foundations of effective negotiations. With these strategies at your disposal, you may confidently negotiate a fair wage and obtain the payment you are due.

Chapter 6

How to Establish Your Firm

Starting your own business may be a thrilling and successful endeavor. It gives you the freedom to follow your passion, express your creativity, and decide how your career will develop. But building a successful business needs thorough preparation, wise judgment, and rigorous execution. We will walk you through the essential processes of starting your own business in this chapter, from conception to execution.

1. Describe Your Goals

Defining your vision is essential before starting the process of starting your own business. Think about the market demand for your services or products, your areas of experience, and your hobbies. Your firm's mission, values, and long-term objectives should be clearly stated. A clear vision will act as a lighthouse for the entire process.

2. Carry Out Market Analysis

To evaluate the viability and potential success of your company, thorough market research is important. Determine who your target market is, learn about their wants, and assess the market for competitors. You may differentiate yourself from other companies in the industry by identifying your unique selling proposition (USP) with the use of this study.

3. Create a Business Plan.

The success of your business is mapped out in a thorough business strategy. Describe the structure, services or goods, target market, marketing goals, financial forecasts, and expansion strategies of your company. Your business plan will operate as a road map for luring investors, obtaining finance, and making wise company decisions.

4. Legal Points to Consider

Initiating a business necessitates various legal issues. Choose your company's legal structure, such as a corporation, limited liability company (LLC), partnership, or sole proprietorship. Register the name of your business, get the required licenses and permissions, and abide by all local, state, and federal laws. To be sure you follow all legal obligations, seek legal advice.

5. Reliable Credit

Your business's ability to succeed depends on your ability to determine its financial needs and secure sufficient finance. Analyze your projected cash flow, ongoing costs, and startup costs. Investigate your financial possibilities, including savings, grants, loans, and investments from partners or venture capitalists. Make a financial strategy that takes your company's early setup and operational requirements into account.

6. Create a Team

For your company to expand and remain viable, you must assemble a capable and committed workforce. Determine the essential positions that are needed to run your company, such as managers, technicians, marketers, and administrators. Identify candidates who fit the culture and values of your company and have the necessary skills and expertise. Encourage innovation and personal development by fostering a cooperative and inclusive work environment.

7. Create Operational Procedures.

Creating effective operational processes is crucial to the seamless operation of your business. Establish standard operating procedures (SOPs), define your workflow, and put in place reliable project management and communication solutions. Utilize technology and automation solutions to improve customer experience, increase productivity, and streamline business processes.

8. Branding and Marketing

To raise awareness, draw in customers, and establish a solid reputation for your company, effective marketing and branding techniques are crucial. Create a memorable brand identity for your business, complete with a logo, tagline, and visual components that appeal to your target market and reflect the values of your company. Use social media, digital platforms, content marketing, and networking opportunities as part of a multi-channel marketing strategy to promote your business.

9. Management of Client Relationships and Client Acquisition

The success of your business depends on attracting clients and keeping reliable bonds. Create a client acquisition approach that is in line with your target market after identifying your ideal clients. offer superior customer service, go above and above for clients, and promote long-term relationships. CRM solutions should be used to keep track of client interactions and customize your communications.

10. Constant Learning and Adjustment

As a business owner, it is imperative to keep up with industry trends and adjust to shifting market conditions because the business landscape is constantly changing. Invest in ongoing education, go to conferences, join associations for professionals, and network with industry leaders. To secure your company's long-term growth and sustainability, embrace innovation, get input from customers and staff, and make wise decisions.

Creating your own business involves a combination of enthusiasm, forethought, and tenacity. You can build a strong foundation for a prosperous corporation by following the steps mentioned in this chapter and utilizing your skills and abilities. Keep in mind that creating a company is a journey, and it is crucial to continue to be flexible, adaptive, and dedicated to constant improvement. You can turn your vision into a prosperous reality if you have the appropriate perspective and use a thoughtful strategy.

www.ingramcontent.com/pod-product-compliance
Lightning Source LLC
Chambersburg PA
CBHW070852220526
45466CB00005B/1969